Instant MuseScore

Learn to create beautiful scores and quality sheet music with this popular, free music composition software

Maxwell Shinn

BIRMINGHAM - MUMBAI

Instant MuseScore

First published: August 2013

Production Reference: 1240813

Published by Packt Publishing Ltd.
Livery Place
35 Livery Street
Birmingham B3 2PB, UK.

ISBN 978-1-78355-936-7

www.packtpub.com

Credits

Author

Maxwell Shinn

Reviewer

Nicolas Froment

Acquisition Editor

Pramila Balan

Commissioning Editor

Sruthi Kutty

Technical Editor

Shali Sasidharan

Project Coordinator

Amey Sawant

Proofreader

Maria Gould

Production Coordinator

Nilesh R. Mohite

Cover Work

Nilesh R. Mohite

Cover Image

Disha Haria

About the Author

Maxwell Shinn is a composer currently located in the Minneapolis region. He first discovered MuseScore in 2009, and shortly thereafter began using it as his exclusive music notation software package. Later, he began contributing to the community by compiling the GNU/Linux nightly builds. Max has composed two full length musicals in MuseScore, as well as works for orchestra, concert band, chamber ensemble, instrumental solo, and others.

Additionally, Max is known for releasing his works to the public, allowing for unlimited performance, recording, and even modification under the Creative Commons BY-SA license. These works are available for download from his website, www.MaxShinnPotential.com.

Acknowledgments

I would like to thank my family and friends for their love and support. Thank you to *Nicolas Froment* and *Mary Finta* for reviewing the drafts of this work, and to *Clarence Lehman* for his guidance in the early stages of this process.

I would also especially like to thank my music composition mentor *Carol Barnett*, without whom I would likely not be composing today. Her patience, kindness, and enthusiasm throughout the years I studied with her have changed me both inside and outside the concert hall.

Additionally, thank you to *Werner Schweer* and many other MuseScore contributors who have given their time and talents to produce such a wonderful piece of software.

Finally, I thank you, the reader, for actually reading the acknowledgments section full of people who you don't know.

About the Reviewer

Nicolas Froment (@lasconic) is a software developer and drummer from Toulouse, France. For the past 10 years he has been working on several music notation related software projects.

As a free software proponent, Nicolas started contributing to MuseScore in 2008 and quickly became one of the main developers. In 2010, he founded the MuseScore company with *Thomas Bonte*, and *Werner Schweer*, the lead developer of MuseScore. He serves as MuseScore's CTO and manages the MuseScore contributor community.

Nicolas wrote and translated a large part of MuseScore official documentation into French.

www.packtpub.com

Support files, eBooks, discount offers and more

You might want to visit www.packtpub.com for support files and downloads related to your book.

Did you know that Packt offers eBook versions of every book published, with PDF and ePub files available? You can upgrade to the eBook version at www.packtpub.com and as a print book customer, you are entitled to a discount on the eBook copy. Get in touch with us at service@packtpub.com for more details.

At www.packtpub.com, you can also read a collection of free technical articles, sign up for a range of free newsletters and receive exclusive discounts and offers on Packt books and eBooks.

packtlib.packtpub.com

Do you need instant solutions to your IT questions? PacktLib is Packt's online digital book library. Here, you can access, read and search across Packt's entire library of books.

Why Subscribe?

- ✦ Fully searchable across every book published by Packt
- ✦ Copy and paste, print and bookmark content
- ✦ On demand and accessible via web browser

Free Access for Packt account holders

If you have an account with Packt at www.packtpub.com, you can use this to access PacktLib today and view nine entirely free books. Simply use your login credentials for immediate access.

Table of Contents

Instant MuseScore

Welcome to Instant MuseScore. This book has been especially created to provide you with all the information that you need to notate music in MuseScore. You will discover the basics of MuseScore, learn to engrave a full score, and finally create parts for individual musicians.

This document contains the following sections:

So, what is MuseScore? describes what MuseScore actually is, what you can do with it, and why it's so great.

Installation teaches you how to download and install MuseScore with minimum fuss and then set it up so that you can use it as soon as possible on Windows, Mac, and GNU/Linux platforms.

Quick start – creating your first score shows you how to navigate the interface, notate notes and rhythms (including ties and triplets), play back your music, copy and paste measures, and print your score.

Top 5 features you need to know about helps you to learn how to perform five common music notation tasks with MuseScore. By the end of this section you will be able to create complete, professional looking parts for any score. This section includes explanations for the following:

- ✦ Adding articulations, dynamics, and text: This shows how to add common markings to your score, such as dynamics, single note articulations, and multi-note articulations.
- ✦ Text: Learn how to insert many different types of text, including:
    - ○ General text
    - ○ Tempo markings
    - ○ Chords symbols
    - ○ Lyrics

- Changing the time and key signature: Here, we see how to change the time signature and the key signature. We will also learn how to deal with transposing instruments.

- Modifying the layout: Figure out how to make your score more readable by musicians. This includes:

    ○ Rehearsal letters

    ○ Barlines

    ○ Stretching and page layout

    ○ Spacers

    ○ Grouping instruments with brackets (and connecting barlines)

    ○ Line/page breaks

    ○ Music size

- Extracting parts: This shows how to go from a score showing all of the parts, to showing the individual parts for musicians.

People and places you should get to know points out a few useful resources, such as the following:

- The MuseScore online users manual

- The MuseScore forums

- MuseScore.com score sharing service

- Advanced how-to page on `musescore.org`

- MuseScore Twitter page

So, what is MuseScore?

MuseScore is a convenient tool that allows you to quickly and easily create beautiful-looking sheet music. Why might this be important?

✦ Engraving music that has been written by hand

✦ Composing directly onto the computer

✦ Transcribing jazz solos from a recording

✦ Archiving sheet music in a freely-accessible digital form

✦ Arranging music for a small ensemble

✦ Recreating lost or damaged parts from a score

✦ Transposing existing music into another key

✦ Creating lead sheets for new or well-known charts

MuseScore has all of the major features that popular music composition packages have, and can be downloaded at no cost. Thus, friends and colleagues don't need to purchase a music composition package in order to be able to see or hear your music. As can be expected from music notation software, MuseScore offers a host of options for playing back your music and exporting it to other formats. Furthermore, if you can program and would like to help develop MuseScore, it is open to contributions from anybody. Because of this, MuseScore is called **libre software**.

MuseScore supports many features that are only found in some of the most expensive music composition packages, such as swing style playback, coda systems, beaming across staves, multiple voices, MIDI input, MusicXML import and export, tempo and intensity changes in real-time, drum sets, concert pitch display, multi-measure rests, and part extraction. Though not all of these more advanced features will be discussed here, information is available online through the links given at the end of the book.

While the history of computing has been defined by word processing and text editing, it didn't take long for people to realize that it was possible to process printed music on a computer, too. Several notable methods for creating printed music from computers emerged early on; however, musicians who wanted a libre, easy to use, low-cost engraving solution were out of luck. In 2002, MuseScore was created for GNU/Linux by *Werner Schweer* using the existing (yet limited) music notation capability of the synthesizer MusE. Joined by *Thomas Bonte* and *Nicolas Froment* in 2008, MuseScore was ported to Windows and Mac, and the present website (www.MuseScore. org) was unveiled to the public. MuseScore's popularity continued to grow as it established itself as a powerful solution for notating music. In 2010, MuseScore Connect was officially announced, making it easy for composers to share their music online and receive feedback from others. Today, MuseScore has grown to be one of the most popular solutions for digital music notation.

MuseScore has been used for several large and small scale projects. Some have used MuseScore to write symphonies, musicals, or video game scores. Others have used it for lead sheets, piano solos, or gifts for loved ones. Many companies, universities, and professional musicians depend on MuseScore for their day-to-day operations. It was used recently to prepare new public domain editions of Bach's Goldberg Variations, available at `www.OpenGoldbergVariations.org`. Since MuseScore can be modified by others, it has been also been used as a base to create software for experimental forms of music notation.

The figures in this book and the compositions they depict are available under the **Creative Commons BY-SA** license, which means anybody may view, modify, and distribute them, as long as the author is credited. (See `CreativeCommons.org` for more information.) The images and MuseScore files are posted online at `www.MaxShinnPotential.com`.

Installation

MuseScore can be installed on Windows, Mac, GNU/Linux, or *BSD. For the scope of this book, I will only discuss Windows, Mac, and Debian-based GNU/Linux distributions (such as Ubuntu, Mint, Bodhi, and so on). For information about how to install MuseScore on other platforms, see `http://musescore.org/en/download`. For this book, I used MuseScore 1.3.

Windows

Installing MuseScore on Windows is similar to installing any other Windows application.

Step 1 – downloading MuseScore

To install MuseScore on Windows, first download the appropriate version for your edition of Windows from `http://musescore.org/en/download`. Usually, the first link underneath the Windows logo should work. Don't worry about the MSI package or the portable version, as they are not needed.

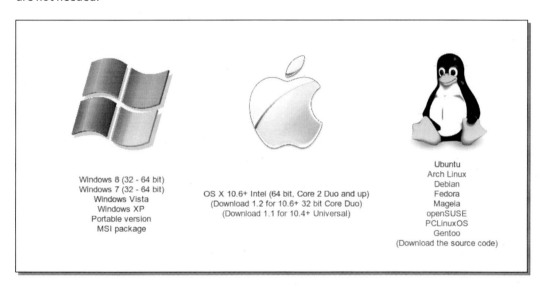

Windows 8 (32 - 64 bit)
Windows 7 (32 - 64 bit)
Windows Vista
Windows XP
Portable version
MSI package

OS X 10.6+ Intel (64 bit, Core 2 Duo and up)
(Download 1.2 for 10.6+ 32 bit Core Duo)
(Download 1.1 for 10.4+ Universal)

Ubuntu
Arch Linux
Debian
Fedora
Mageia
openSUSE
PCLinuxOS
Gentoo
(Download the source code)

Step 2 – running the installer

After you have downloaded it, find the location where you downloaded the file and double-click on the installer to begin the installation. You can click on the **Next** button on each screen until you see the button labeled **Install**. Click on this button, and MuseScore will be installed. Once you see the **Finish** button, it means that MuseScore has been successfully installed, and you can click on this button to exit the installer.

Now, you can start MuseScore by going to the Start menu, and going to **All Programs**, then **MuseScore**, and finally clicking on **MuseScore**.

Mac OS X

Installation on a Mac is as easy as dragging-and-dropping.

Step 1 – downloading MuseScore

First, go to the download page (`http://musescore.org/en/download`) and download the appropriate version for your Mac. If you have Version 10.6 or newer, use the 10.6+ version. Note that you may need to install a different version if you have a 32-bit processor or an older version of OS X. If in doubt, and you have a newer Mac, try the 64-bit Core 2 Duo version. (If the version you download doesn't work, you can always download a different one!)

Step 2 – installing it on your computer

Once you download it, run the file. You should see a large icon appear. Drag this item to your `Applications` folder. It may ask you for a password; if so, enter it and click on **Authenticate**. This will install MuseScore to your computer.

Now that it is installed, to run MuseScore, navigate to the `Applications` folder and click on the MuseScore icon.

GNU/Linux

MuseScore is available in most distributions' package managers, or by following these instructions for Debian-based distributions.

Step 1 – installing MuseScore through your package manager

To install MuseScore on a Debian-based GNU/Linux distribution, open a terminal, such as Konsole, xterm, or the GNOME Terminal, and type the following:

```
sudo apt-get install musescore
```

Then hit *Return*. When prompted, press *Y* and hit *Return* again, and MuseScore will be installed.

Once installed, MuseScore can be run through your application menu or by typing `musescore` into the terminal and pressing *Return*.

And that's it

We had a look at the steps involved in installing MuseScore for different operating systems. By this point, you should have a working installation of MuseScore. So what are we waiting for? It's time to play around and discover more about it!

Quick start – creating your first score

Now that MuseScore is installed, let's get started on creating our first score.

Step 1 – navigating the interface

When you first open MuseScore, you should see the following screen:

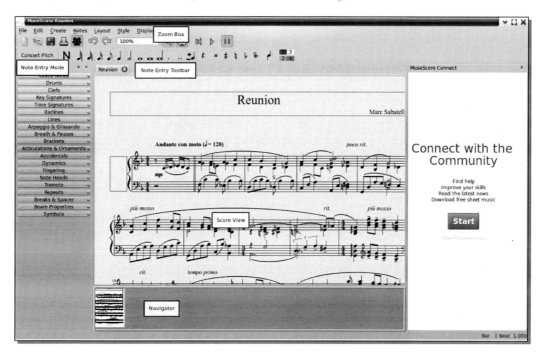

That's good! For now, let's hit the **X** in the upper-right corner of the section entitled **MuseScore Connect**. **MuseScore Connect** is a useful tool that allows you to share scores online with friends or colleagues, and explore scores from others. Once you close it, you can open it again at any time by going to the **Display** menu and clicking on **MuseScore Connect**. While we will not be discussing it in this book, you are encouraged to explore what it has to offer as you learn more about MuseScore.

Since the demo score has been opened for us, let's figure out how to navigate scores in MuseScore. The current score will always be visible in the **Score View**, the section of the screen that shows the score you're currently editing. You can zoom in and out of the Score View by using the drop-down box in the toolbar called the **Zoom Box**. Initially, this is set to **100%**, but can be changed easily by either typing in a new percentage and pressing *Return*, or using the drop-down menu to select a new zoom amount. Let's change it to **150%** using either of these methods. It is also possible to zoom in and out by holding *Ctrl* (or ⌘ on Mac) and moving the scroll wheel on your mouse.

Note that Mac users should always use the ⌘ key instead of the *Ctrl* key. The *Ctrl* key is used throughout the book because it applies to both Windows and GNU/Linux. However, anytime the *Ctrl* key is indicated, Mac users should use the ⌘ key instead.

Now we are zoomed in, but we may not be looking at what we would like to look at. Click and hold anywhere on the score, as long as it is not on top of any markings. Then, when you drag the mouse, you will be able to move the score. Using your mouse's scroll wheel without the *Ctrl* (or ⌘) key pressed will move the score vertically, and holding *Shift* while scrolling will move it horizontally.

Though the sample score is not very long, the bar along the bottom of the screen with a miniature version of the score is another convenient way to navigate. This bar is called the **Navigator**. Clicking-and-dragging the blue box in the Navigator will change the portion of the score that can be seen in the Score View. This allows you to jump around to other portions of the score quickly when dealing with long scores. By clicking-and-dragging the border between this and the Score View, we can also adjust the size of both relative to each other.

Step 2 – creating a score

Let's make our first piece! To start, go to the **File** menu at the top of the screen and select **New**. You will be prompted for some basic information about the piece, such as the composer's name and the title of the piece. Note that all of the information on this screen is optional. Once you have filled in the relevant boxes, click the **Next** button.

The next screen will prompt you about which instruments to add. You can find the correct instruments by clicking on the appropriate family of instruments on the side of the dialog box, such as **Strings**. Clicking on the instrument will add it to your list. Let's add a piano (under **Keyboards**) and then a trombone (under **Brass**) for practice. As you add instruments, they will appear on the right-hand side of the dialog box. The order of this list will also be the order of your score. If you would like the instruments to be in a different order in the score, you can select an instrument in the list and click on the **Up** or **Down** button. Let's move the trombone above the piano by selecting it and clicking on the **Up** button. Don't worry, if you need to add more instruments later, you can return to this dialog at any time by selecting **Instruments** under the **Create** menu on the main screen.

 If you wish to see rare instruments as well, you can click on the **Show more** checkbox to view additional instruments.

After you have finished selecting your instruments, click on the **Next** button. You will be prompted for a key signature. Hitting **Next** again will prompt you for the time signature and number of measures. Of course, it is also possible to insert measures and change the time or key signature throughout the piece. For our sample piece, let's leave all of these at their defaults.

When you are done, hit the **Finish** button. MuseScore will create a score for you that looks like the following screenshot:

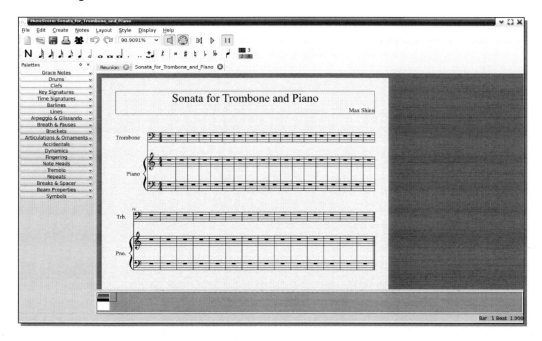

Notice how our piece has created a new tab near the top of the screen. Tabs are an easy way of managing all of the files you have open at any given time. Clicking on one of the tabs will allow you to work on that piece of music.

Step 3 – entering notes

In order to enter notes into our score, we need to enter **Note Entry mode**. MuseScore has various modes that we can use to accomplish special tasks. You can enter Note Entry mode by clicking on the **N** button in the toolbar. You can tell whether you are in Note Entry mode at any given time by checking whether the **N** button is depressed. You may also enter/exit Note Entry mode by pressing the *N* key.

After you enter Note Entry mode, the quarter note should be selected by default. If you hover over the staff, you should see a light blue outline of a note appear. Clicking here will cause a quarter note of that pitch to be inserted. In the toolbar, you will see several notes of different lengths, such as half notes, eighth notes, and whole notes. This area is called the **Note Entry toolbar,** and indicates which note will be inserted when you click on the staff. Right now, the quarter note should be selected. Click on the half note, and then click an area of the staff on top of the rest that is immediately after the quarter note we just inserted. A half note of the pitch you chose will be added.

In MuseScore, whenever we add notes, we must overwrite other notes. First, we overwrote a whole rest with a quarter note, which caused three beats of rest to be added after the quarter note. Then, we overwrote a quarter rest with a half note. Since the half note was longer than the quarter rest, it also overwrote one beat from the half rest following it, and changed the rest to a quarter rest to accommodate the size of the half note.

To add an accidental, simply insert the note without the accidental, and then press the appropriate accidental button in the toolbar. For example, let's insert an F♯ eighth note. We click on the eighth note button, then on the F line of the staff, and finally on the sharp button in the toolbar.

We can insert dotted notes in a similar fashion by using the dot button on the Note Entry toolbar. In the next measure, let's add a G dotted quarter note by clicking on the quarter note in the Note Entry toolbar, then clicking on the dot button, and then clicking on a G in the staff. The dot will stay selected after you insert the note. If you would like to deselect the dot, you can click on it again. It is also automatically deselected when you change the note duration. Thus, you should always select the dot after you select the value of the note you would like to be dotted.

It is possible to notate more quickly using keyboard shortcuts. The number keys *1* through *9* will select different durations, and the letters *A* through *G* will insert the designated note. The *o* key inserts a rest. Inserting notes this way will always insert the closest note with the desired pitch. If you hold *Ctrl* (or ⌘ on Mac) while pressing the up or down arrow keys, MuseScore will move the last note you inserted up or down an octave. So, inserting a C half note and moving it up an octave can be accomplished by pressing the sequence *6 C Ctrl + ↑*. Notes can be adjusted by a half step by pressing the up or down arrows without holding the *Ctrl* key. Hitting the up arrow will always create sharps, and the down arrow creates flats. This allows us to insert an F♯ eighth note with the keystroke sequence *4 f ↑*.

 While at first the keyboard shortcuts may seem complicated, as you get the hang of MuseScore, it is worthwhile to learn them. They will allow you to notate music extremely quickly and make your overall experience with MuseScore much more pleasurable.

Making chords is also very straightforward. We just click on top of our previously inserted note after selecting a note of the same value. Be careful! If a different note length is selected, it will overwrite the previous note.

Chords can also be inserted rapidly with keyboard shortcuts. Just start by inserting the first note of the chord normally. If you would like to insert a note of the chord above the previous note, hold *Alt* and press the interval above the previous note you would like to insert. To insert it below, hold *Shift* and do the same. Notes are always inserted in the present key signature. So to insert a C first inversion chord, press the sequence *E Alt + 3 Alt + 4*, or to insert a C second inversion chord, press the sequence *G Alt + 4 Alt + 3*. Alternatively, after inserting the first note, you can hold *Shift* and type the letter names of the notes to add to the chord. So pressing the sequence *G Shift+C Shift+E* would insert the same C second inversion chord.

If you ever make a mistake, you can always undo your latest changes by going to the **Edit** menu and selecting **Undo**. You can also use the keyboard shortcut *Ctrl + Z* (or ⌘ + *Z* on Mac).

Let's put some notes and chords in some measures for both the trombone and piano parts so that we have something to work with.

Inserting triplets

To insert a triplet, first enter Note Entry mode. Then, from the Note Entry toolbar, choose the total duration that you would like all three triplets to sum to. Next, insert the first note of the triplet in the position you would like the triplet to occupy. After this, exit Note Entry mode, and from the **Notes** menu, under the **Tuplets** submenu, click on the **Triplet** option. A triplet will be created with the selected note as the first note. MuseScore will automatically enter Note Entry mode for you again, and select the correct duration of note needed to complete the triplet. From here, you can replace the two rests with notes by inserting the correct notes on top of them, as we did when we entered notes previously.

Also, there is a keyboard shortcut to make this process easier. While in Note Entry mode, select the proper duration you would like the entire triplet to be, as before, but then hit *Ctrl + 3* (or ⌘ + *3* on Mac). The triplet will be inserted, and the proper note duration to fill in the triplet will be selected. You can now enter the notes of the triplet as you would enter normal notes. For instance, to insert a triplet arpeggio of an F major triad totaling one beat, we would press the sequence *5 Ctrl + 3 F A C*. For a B major triad totaling two beats, we would similarly press *6 Ctrl + 3 B D↑F↑*.

Inserting ties

Ties are very easy to create in MuseScore. The simplest way to insert a tie is to insert both of the notes that you want to be tied together, exit Note Entry mode, click on the first note, and then click on the tie button in the toolbar, or press the + key. Make sure the two notes you are trying to tie together have the same pitch, or no tie will be inserted. This method works for individual notes, and also for chords. In order to have flexibility when tying chords, you must tie each note of the chord individually if you want the full chord to be tied. An easy way to do this is to ensure that you are not in Note Entry mode, hold *Shift*, click on the first note of the first chord so that the whole chord is selected, and press the + key. Again, for this to work, you must have two chords with identical pitches next to each other.

If you are working with keyboard shortcuts, then there is also a faster way to enter ties that does not require the use of the mouse. After you enter a note in Note Entry mode, the note you just entered will be selected, and the cursor will be located on the right-hand side of this note, as shown in the following screenshot:

Then, using the appropriate keyboard shortcut, select the duration of note you would like this note to be tied to. Finally, press the + key. MuseScore will insert a note of the selected duration tied to the previous note. So, pressing the sequence *5 C 4 +* will insert a quarter note C tied to an eighth note. While this method is extremely convenient for single notes, it does not work for chords.

Often, it is necessary to flip the tie for visual appeal, especially when tying chords. This can be accomplished by ensuring that you are not in Note Entry mode, clicking on a tie, and then pressing the *X* key.

 Even though ties look very similar to slurs in many situations, they are created differently. Slurs will be discussed later.

Copying and pasting

Suppose that we would like to repeat a measure in the bass line, or that the next measure in the melody is very similar to the previous measure. As in a word processor, we can copy and paste measures and fragments of music.

First, let's copy and paste a measure. Exit Note Entry mode by ensuring the **N** button in the toolbar is not selected. Then, click on a portion of the measure where no notes are present. The measure should be selected, as indicated by the blue box around it. Now, either go to the **Edit** menu and click on **Copy**, or press *Ctrl + C* (⌘ + C on Mac). The measure will be copied to the clipboard. Now, click on a portion of the target measure without any notes, and either click on **Paste** from the **Edit** menu, or press *Ctrl + V* (⌘ + V on Mac). The notes will be inserted, and the target measure will be overwritten.

It is also possible to copy any portion of your score, even if it spans partial measures or multiple staves. First, click on the note at the top-left of the region you want to copy. In the following example, this would be the E ♭ in the right hand. Then, press and hold the *Shift* key, and click on the note at the bottom right corner of the region you would like to copy. Here, that would be the D in the left hand. MuseScore will select all of the notes in between.

Once you have selected the region, you can copy it in the same way you copied the measure before. To paste the region, click on the first note or rest in the uppermost stave where you would like to paste it, and paste as we did with a single measure using either *Ctrl + V* or **Paste** from the **Edit** menu. If your selection has different measure breaks or is in a different meter than the destination, the selection will be reflowed to fit the destination, and ties will be added as necessary.

Inserting and deleting measures

Often, it is helpful to insert or delete a measure in your score. Luckily, MuseScore makes this extremely easy. To insert a measure, select the measure (as we did when we copied a measure) immediately after the location where you would like to insert the measure. Then, go to the **Create** menu, and under the **Measures** submenu, select **Insert Measure**. A measure will be inserted. To insert multiple measures, select **Insert Measures**. A dialog box will prompt you for how many measures to insert.

If you would like to add measures to the end of the score, you can select **Append Measures** from under the **Measures** submenu within the **Create** menu. There is no need to select any measures to perform this operation.

To delete measures, simply select the measure by clicking any blank area within the measure, and then go to the **Edit** menu, and click on **Delete Selected Measures**. Doing so will delete this measure position within all staves, not just the selected staff. You can also select multiple measures (as we did earlier when we were copying by selecting one measure, holding the *Shift* key, and selecting additional measures), and use the same menu button to delete all of the measures that you have selected.

Step 4 – playing back your music

After we continue along in this way for a while, we may be ready to hear our work played back by the computer. This is as easy as clicking the ‣ button in the toolbar, or pressing the space bar. Pressing either again will stop playback.

If you would like to hear only a portion of the piece played back, exit Note Entry mode by clicking on the **N** button in the toolbar, or by pressing the *N* key on the keyboard. Then, click on the note you would like to start with. (A note from any instrument will work.) When you press play, MuseScore will automatically play back the piece from this point.

It should also be noted that while your score is playing back, you are free to zoom in and out, to move the page up and down with your mouse's scroll wheel, and to move left and right by holding the *Shift* key while using the scroll wheel. Unfortunately, you cannot adjust the score by dragging the mouse during playback.

You can also selectively mute and adjust the balance of different instruments during playback. Let's mute the trombone so that we only hear the piano part right now. Go to the **Display** menu, and click on the **Mixer** option. You should be presented with the following screen:

If we click on the **Mute** checkbox near the **Trombone** label, when we play back the piece, we will not be able to hear the trombone. Unchecking it will restore the trombone's sound. We can also change the balance of the different instruments by adjusting the **Vol** dial. To adjust the dial, click on it and hold, and then drag your mouse cursor *straight up* to increase the volume or *straight down* to decrease it. These settings can also be adjusted while the piece is playing back, allowing you to easily fine-tune the balance. You can close this window when you no longer need it.

Step 5 – printing and exporting your music

Printing your piece is as simple as going to the **File** menu and pressing the **Print** menu option. It will print exactly as it is displayed on the page. We will discuss how to print separate parts from the full score later.

However, it is also possible to save your piece as an audio file (which will sound exactly as MuseScore's playback sounds), a PDF, or a MusicXML file, which can be imported into other notation software. To do this, under the **File** menu, select **Save a Copy**. MuseScore has the ability to save audio files in MIDI, Wave, Ogg Vorbis, and FLAC formats, in addition to MusicXML and PDF. Due to patent restrictions, exporting to MP3 is not possible, and MP3s have to be created by converting the Wave or FLAC file to MP3. Choose the file type you would like from the **Filter** drop-down box, and click on the **Save** button.

Top 5 features you need to know about

Now that we can enter notes and rhythms, let's learn how to add other musical elements to our score.

Articulations and dynamics

Let's look at how to insert dynamics and different types of articulations.

Single-note articulations

MuseScore makes adding articulations very easy! First, locate the palette. In the upcoming section, you will become very accustomed to using the palette, as it can be used to insert most of the non-note entities in your score. The palette is divided into several sections, which you can see in the following screenshot. To access the features of each section, simply click on it from within the palette.

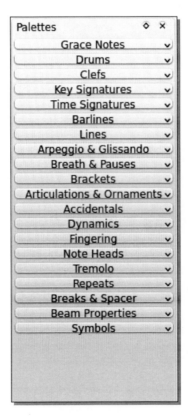

To insert articulations, we will be using the section of the palette labeled **Articulations & Ornaments**. Click on this part of the palette, and several articulations will show up. Now, you can just drag-and-drop the articulation you would like onto any note. As you hover over the note before you drop the articulation, the note will turn red, as shown in the following screenshot:

Once you drop it onto the note, MuseScore will automatically position the articulation above or below the note.

Alternatively, if you dislike the drag-and-drop approach, you may also use the following procedure. Simply ensure that you are not in Note Entry mode, click on any note, and double-click on the articulation in the palette that you would like to insert.

If you want to insert an articulation on a chord, you only need to select one note in the chord. It doesn't matter which note you select. MuseScore will recognize that it is part of a chord, and position it correctly.

Sometimes, you may notice that MuseScore does not automatically position the articulations how you would like. You can move any articulation by ensuring that you are not in Note Entry mode, and then clicking-and-dragging the articulation on the score.

Dynamics

Inserting dynamics is very similar to inserting articulations. Instead of finding the **Articulations & Ornaments** section, we instead go to the **Dynamics** section.

To insert a dynamic marking, just drag-and-drop it onto the score. However, unlike articulations, MuseScore will not automatically position dynamics when you drag-and-drop them. They will be inserted at the location where they are dropped. Because it can be ambiguous what note the dynamic should be attached to, MuseScore will indicate this by drawing a line from the dynamic to the note before you drop it onto the score, as shown in following figure. The note that it is attached to is called the **Anchor**.

It is important to choose the correct anchor. MuseScore continuously re-adjusts the layout to make sure your music looks good, and sometimes this involves moving measures to new lines. Choosing the right anchor will ensure that the dynamic always follows the anchor note.

MuseScore also has the ability to automatically position dynamics, as it did with the articulations. Similarly to articulations, this can be accomplished by checking to make sure that you are not in Note Entry mode, clicking on any note in the score, and then double-clicking on a dynamic from the palette.

If you need to adjust the position of the dynamic after you insert it, you can drag-and-drop it to wherever you would like, just as we did with articulations. When you do this, the anchor will not change.

You can find more dynamics and dynamic-like articulations (such as fortepiano) by going to the **Create** menu, and under **Text**, clicking on **Dynamics**. These can be inserted by either double-clicking on them or dragging them to the score, just like those from the palette. To insert one not found in either location, start by choosing any of the dynamics (it doesn't matter which one) in the palette, and inserting it into the score. Double-click on the newly inserted dynamic, and a text editing box will appear. From here, you can type in the dynamic you would like. We will learn more about inserting text soon!

Hairpins, slurs, ottava brackets, and pedal markings

Some symbols in music notation span multiple notes. Luckily, MuseScore has a uniform way of entering these into your score. Because they have a starting point and an ending point, each of these symbols is connected to two anchors rather than one. They start at the first anchor and end at the second. Hence, we need to deal with these slightly differently than normal articulations.

Hairpins (**crescendos** and **diminuendos**) are similar to dynamics in that, when you drag them onto the score, they will appear in the same position where you drop them. You will see a line connecting your mouse to one of the notes, as we saw when inserting dynamics. The line shows the first anchor the hairpin is connected to. The second anchor will be automatically chosen to be the first note of the next measure. To insert a hairpin, click on the **Lines** section of the palette, and then drag-and-drop it into the score.

However, let's suppose we want the hairpin to span two measures instead. It is very simple to change the second anchor. Double-click on the slur. This will enter Edit mode. Most elements have an Edit mode that allows adjustments to be made to them, but the hairpin Edit mode is especially useful. Once we enter the hairpin's Edit mode, we will see two small squares appear. The one on the right will be selected automatically, as shown in the following figure:

Since the second box is selected, we can adjust the second anchor by pressing *Shift +* → to move it one note to the right, or *Shift +* ← to move it one note to the left. This will change the note that the second anchor is connected to, and re-adjust the hairpin's size. When we are done, we can click anywhere else on the score to exit Edit mode.

The same technique can be used for adjusting the first anchor if you change your mind after inserting the hairpin. After entering Edit mode, just click on the first box to select it. Then, *Shift +* → and *Shift +* ← will adjust the first anchor instead. It is important to use this method instead of just dragging the boxes, as dragging the boxes will not change the anchors.

Slurs, pedal markings, and **ottava brackets** can be entered exactly the same way. Simply find the appropriate item in the **Lines** section of the palette, drag them to the appropriate starting note, and adjust the anchors through Edit mode if necessary.

One issue with slurs is that, in addition to specifying the two notes they connect, it is often necessary to also specify their shape. To change the shape, insert the slur in the same way we inserted the hairpin. Then enter Edit mode by double-clicking on the slur. Instead of two boxes, four boxes will appear. Clicking-and-dragging the two middle boxes will change the shape of the slur by stretching it in the direction you drag the boxes. It is often necessary to play around with the boxes a bit to find the desired shape.

Additionally, there are keyboard shortcuts that can make the process of inserting slurs and hairpins easier. First, make sure you are not in Note Entry mode. Then, click on the note that you would like to make the first anchor. Next, press and hold *Ctrl* (⌘ on Mac). While holding it down, click the note you would like to make the second anchor. When both notes are selected, let go of the *Ctrl* key. To insert a slur between these notes, press the *S* key. To insert a crescendo, press *H*. To insert a diminuendo, press *Shift + H*.

Text

Almost all scores include some markings that use text. Whether it is a tempo marking, stylistic indicator, or rehearsal letter, text is a necessary component for any score.

General text

There are four different types of text types that we will discuss. The most basic type is **Staff Text**. As the name implies, staff text applies to only one staff. It is useful for things that only apply to one instrument's part, such as writing "pizzicato" or "simile". Later, we will learn to create individual parts for each instrument. Staff text will only appear on the part containing the staff where it was inserted. This allows you to specify "Follow conductor" only on the viola part, for instance.

System Text is similar to staff text, except that when we extract parts, it will be included in all the parts. It should be used for things that all musicians should see, such as "molto rit." or "colla voce". Normally, these should be inserted on the top staff line.

A **Rehearsal Mark** is a special type of system text. Rehearsal marks are displayed in a larger font and surrounded by a box, and should be used for rehearsal letters. They should also generally be inserted on the uppermost staff.

Like articulations, text elements must be attached to an anchor note. To insert one of these three types of text, first ensure you are not in Note Entry mode, and then click on the note that you would like to be the anchor. Then, from the **Create** menu, find the **Text** submenu, and click on either **Staff Text, System Text,** or **Rehearsal Mark**. Alternatively, after selecting the anchor, you can press *Ctrl + T* (⌘ + *T* on Mac) to insert **Staff Text,** *Ctrl + Shift + T* (⌘ + *Shift + T* on Mac) to insert **System Text,** or *Ctrl + M* (⌘ + *M* on Mac) to insert a **Rehearsal Mark**. The following screenshot shows staff text:

Now, you can start typing what you would like the text to say. You may notice that the following toolbar appears at the bottom of the screen when you are editing text:

The first button will bring up a selection of text symbols that can be inserted, such as a miniature quarter note or the copyright symbol. The other buttons change the font size, style, and alignment, and should be familiar to you from word processing software. As in a word processor, to change the formatting, you can press one of these buttons and start typing, or highlight some text from what you have typed and click on the appropriate button.

Click anywhere else on the score to finish editing the text. If you would like to make changes at a later time, you can always double-click on the text to edit it again.

Tempo markings

It is also possible to insert **Tempo Markings,** a fourth type of text similar to system text. Tempo markings show up in a different font than system text, but they also allow you to change the tempo of playback. To insert a tempo marking, make sure you are not in Note Entry mode and click on the note you would like to anchor it to. (Generally, it is best to choose a note on the top staff.) Then, either go to the **Create** menu, then the **Text** submenu, and click on **Tempo,** or press *Ctrl + Alt + T* (⌘ *+ Alt + T* on Mac). The following dialog box will appear:

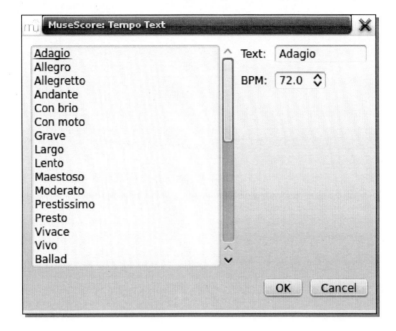

From here, you can select one of the predefined tempos on the left, or create your own by typing the name and number of beats per minute (**BPM**) in the boxes on the right. Then, click on **OK**. The tempo will be inserted. Like the other forms of text, you can edit it by double-clicking on it. You can also change the BPM by right-clicking on the tempo marking and selecting **Tempo Properties**.

The BPM always specifies the number of quarter notes per minute, even when in compound time. Make sure you account for this when setting the tempo in 6/8 passages.

Chord symbols

In jazz and popular music, it is very common to give musicians chord symbols to read from. To create a chord symbol, make sure you are not in Note Entry mode, and click on a note that you would like to add a chord symbol to. Then, either go to the **Create** menu, go to the **Text** submenu, and select **Chord Name**, or press *Ctrl + K* (⌘ *+ K* on Mac). A text box should appear that looks exactly like the ones we saw before. Now, you can type the name of the chord in the same way you would write it on paper. (For example, D minor would be Dm, and a G7 chord would just be G7.) All lowercase *b* characters will be converted into flat signs, and all # characters will be converted into sharps. To move to the next location in the measure, press the space bar. If you press the space bar repeatedly, you will move forward without inserting any chords.

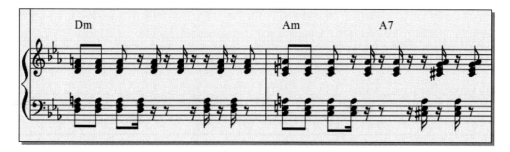

Now that our chords are inserted, we can optionally make them look stylized. To do this, go to the **Style** menu and click on **Edit General Style**. Then, click on the **Chordnames** option on the left-hand side. You should see a textbox appear on the right-hand side containing the text `stdchords.xml`. Change this to `jazzchords.xml`, and then press **OK**. The chords you entered should be appropriately stylized.

Many styles of notation, especially within jazz music, use chord symbols and slashes to indicate improvisation. To create these slashes in MuseScore, insert four quarter notes on the middle line of the staff. Then, after exiting Note Entry mode, right-click on each note and select **Note Properties**. Check the box that says **Stemless**. Also, find the option labeled **velocity type** and choose **user**, and then change the value of the box velocity (0-127) to 0. Now press **OK**. Then, locate the section of the palette labeled **Note Heads,** and drag the parallelogram slash shape on top of each note. This will create the slash notation.

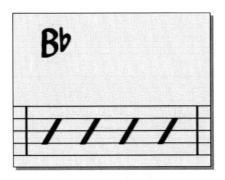

Lyrics

If we want to notate music for voice, it is essential that we are able to add lyrics! Lyrics are tied to individual notes as well. When we insert them, MuseScore will automatically change the layout of our entire score to make sure they are properly spaced.

First, locate the staff you would like to add lyrics to. Then, make sure you are not in Note Entry mode and click on the first note of the line. Now, either go to **Create**, then go to **Text** submenu, and click on **Lyrics**, or press *Ctrl + L* (⌘ *+ L* on Mac). A textbox will appear as shown in the following screenshot:

Then, start typing your first word. To move onto the next note, press the space bar. If there is more than one syllable in your word, press the - key instead of the space bar when you have finished typing the first syllable. This will advance to the next note and insert a hyphen. When a word or syllable is to be held over multiple tied notes, type the word or syllable in the first textbox, and then type an underscore (_) in all of the textboxes over which the note is to be held.

When you are done, click anywhere else on the screen to finish editing the lyrics. To make changes to your lyrics, similarly to other text, just double-click on them.

It is also possible to insert additional verses. Once you have inserted the first verse, make sure you are not in Note Entry mode and click on the first note of the section. Now, either go to the **Create** menu, then go to the **Text** submenu, and click on **Lyrics**, or press *Ctrl + L* (⌘ + *L* on Mac). A new textbox will appear below the previously inserted lyrics as shown in the following figure:

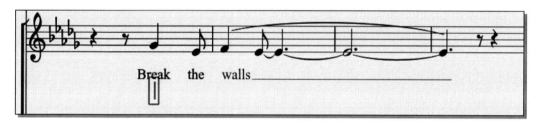

Changing the time and key signature

Now that we can add notes and articulations to our score, let's find out how to change the time and key signature.

Changing the time signature

Changing time signatures in the middle of a piece is as easy as dragging and dropping. First, find the **Time Signatures** section of the palette. To insert one of these time signatures, click-and-drag it from the palette to a measure in the score. The measure should highlight as you hover over it. When you release the mouse button, the time signature at this point will be changed.

If you need a time signature that is not listed in the palette, you can create your own. Under the **Create** menu, click on **Time Signatures**. You will notice on the right-hand side of this dialog box that there are several textboxes separated by + signs, with one more box underneath. To make a time signature, type the time signature into the first box on top and the lower box. For example, let's create a measure of 7/8. First, put the number 7 in the first textbox on top, and then put the number 8 in the textbox at the bottom. All other textboxes can be left at 0. Finally, click on **Add**. The time signature will appear on the left-hand side of the dialog box. It can then be inserted by dragging and dropping it into the score, as we did with the time signatures from the palette.

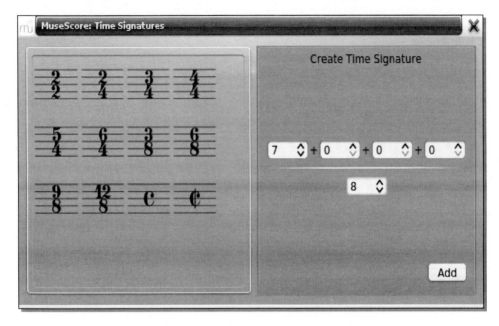

 Be careful if you are changing the time signature of a single measure in the middle of a piece. If you just insert the new time signature, the time signature of all of the later music will be changed. This has the potential to delete some of your work! To avoid this, before you change the time signature, insert a copy of the existing time signature after your desired time signature change, and then insert the new time signature. So for instance, if you have a piece written in 4/4 and would like to insert one measure of 3/4 at measure 17, drag a 4/4 time signature on top of measure 18, and then insert the 3/4 time signature at measure 17. This way, the remainder of your score will not be converted to 3/4.

Changing the key signature

It is very easy to change the key signature in MuseScore. Unlike the time signature, the key signature is set on a per-staff basis. In other words, it is possible to have different instruments playing in different key signatures, an important feature for transposing instruments. Since some parts (notably French horn parts) were traditionally written without a key signature, it also gives you the flexibility between the old and modern styles.

To change the key signature of a staff, first click on the **Key Signatures** section of the palette. You should see several different key signatures to choose from. To add one to the score, click-and-drag it from the palette to the first measure you would like to have this key signature. The measure should highlight as you drag your mouse across it, and when you drop it, the key signature will be changed at the beginning of this measure. You will need to do this for each staff in your score.

Transposing music

MuseScore also has a feature that makes it convenient to transpose sections of music to different keys. To use this feature, select the measures you would like to be transposed, as we did when we were copying and pasting. Then, from the **Notes** menu, select **Transpose**. A dialog box will appear, giving several options.

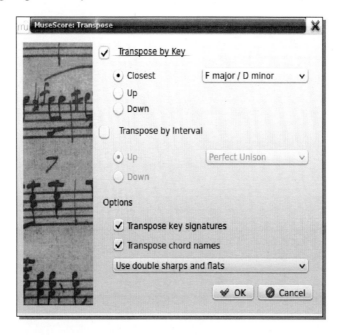

There are two main ways to transpose music: **Transpose by Key**, and **Transpose by Interval**. **Transpose by Key** looks at the key signature the passage is currently in, and uses this to change it to the key you specify. **Transpose by Interval** allows you to transpose all of the notes up or down by any given interval. Select whichever method you would like, and then choose the key signature or interval to transpose to.

There is also a checkbox at the bottom that says **Transpose key signatures**. If this box is checked, MuseScore will change the key signature immediately before the passage begins. If you would like to keep the key signature the same, uncheck this box. When you are finished, click on the **OK** button.

MuseScore differentiates between enharmonic intervals in the same way you would expect it to. For example, if a C♯ is transposed up by a diminished fifth, it will become a G♮; however, if it is transposed up by an augmented fourth, it will become an F𝄪. This behavior can be changed by changing the drop-down box from **Use double sharps and flats** to **Single sharps and flats only** to prefer the simpler enharmonic spellings.

Transposing instruments

The formalities of dealing with transposing instruments frequently cause trouble even for experienced musicians. Besides taking an extra moment to figure out the correct note to write down, it can also make chords harder to read if there are some staves in one key signature and others in a different one.

When you create a score, all instruments will be displayed in the pitch where they will be read by musicians. However, clicking on the **Concert Pitch** button in the toolbar will, as the name implies, transpose all instruments into concert pitch. Clicking on it again will make all transposing instruments return to normal. Just make sure you remember to convert it back into the transposed key signature before printing your score!

Formatting

Since one of the most underestimated jobs of the composer is to make music easily readable for musicians, one of the most important functions of MuseScore is to make your music look nice. While MuseScore can guess many things automatically, it can't guess everything, and it frequently guesses incorrectly. There are many tools that you can use to fix these mistakes, and also add some additional formatting elements to help musicians more easily understand your music.

Barlines and repeats

By default, all barlines consist of just a single line. But MuseScore is capable of more than this! We may find a selection of different possible barlines, including repeat signs, in the section of the palette labeled **Barlines**. Find and click on this section. Click on the barline in the score that you would like to change. It should highlight in blue after you click on it. Then double-click on the type of barline in the palette that you would like to change it to.

Alternatively, if you have a steady hand, you can drag-and-drop a new barline directly onto an existing barline. As you drag the new barline on top of the old one, the old one will highlight in red. If you have changed a barline and wish to change it back, either insert the standard barline at this location to revert back to a normal one, or ensure you are not in Note Entry mode, then click on the modified barline, and press the *Delete* key.

Page layout

There are a few additional aspects that affect how your music will look on the page. The first thing to consider is what type of paper will be used to print your score. MuseScore defaults to A4 paper which, while familiar to European users, may be undesirable for those from North America. Another problem that you may encounter if you work with large scores is sometimes there are too many staves to fit on the page!

To change these settings, go to **Layout** and click on **Page Settings**. To change the type of paper, find the drop-down box in the upper left-hand side of the dialog box that reads **Page Size**, and change it to your desired size. Besides changing it to **Letter** paper, you can also select **Legal** for legal paper or **B5** for marching band sized paper. You can also check the **Landscape** checkbox to change it from portrait to landscape orientation.

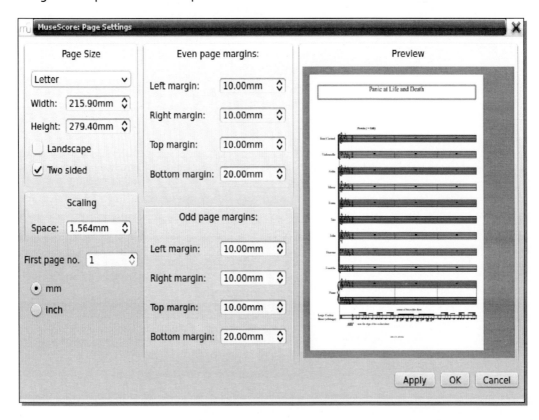

If your score has too many instruments to fit on the page as described previously, you can remedy the problem using this screen. Find the textbox labeled **Space** under the **Scaling** section. This textbox determines the amount of space between two lines on the staff. Changing the value of this to a slightly lower value will cause your music to shrink. MuseScore will automatically adjust the size of all other elements of your score to ensure that they will look normal.

You may notice that you can see a preview of the first page of your score on the right side of the dialog box. When you are satisfied with what you see, click on **OK**, and your score will be updated.

Spacers

Spacers are a unique feature of MuseScore that make avoiding collisions between staves much easier. Suppose you encounter a situation where an element near the bottom of one staff runs into an element from the staff below it.

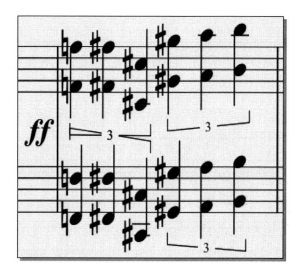

One option is to click-and-drag the offending elements (in this case, the triplet brackets) up or down. However, this often creates awkward looking music. Instead, we can use a **Spacer**. A spacer is a tool that can be used to "push" two staves apart from each other. In other words, it inserts space between any two staves.

To create a spacer, locate the section of the palette labeled **Breaks & Spacer**, and find the ⊤ icon. If this icon can be dragged and dropped on top of a measure, it will sit directly below this measure and allow you to increase the amount of space between that staff and the staff below it.

Let's drag this onto a staff that has another staff underneath it. When you first insert it, it won't really do anything; it will just sit below the staff.

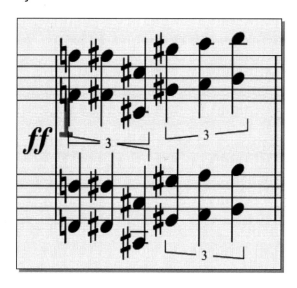

However, if we double-click on it, a small box will appear at the bottom, as shown in the next screenshot. If we click-and-drag this box down, we will see that the spacer expands. When it gets large enough to touch the staff below it, it will "push" it out of the way. Don't worry, when we print our music, the spacers themselves will not show up; they are just tools that we can use to help us adjust the layout. To delete a spacer, click on it once, and press the *Delete* key.

 Later, we will learn how to extract parts. While spacers will extract to the parts, they may no longer be necessary. Don't worry about deleting them if they are no longer useful.

Line and page breaks

It is often useful to be able to specify where we would like the music to break to a new line or page. To do this, find the **Breaks & Spacer** section of the palette. Hovering over each icon in this section of the palette will tell us what it does. We can drag either the line break or page break onto a measure in the score, and the line or page will break immediately after the specified measure. Alternatively, you can click on a barline and press the *Enter* key to insert a line break at this location. While small indicators will appear at the end of the line specifying that a manual line or page break has been inserted, they will not show up when the score is printed. Clicking on this icon once and pressing the *Delete* key will remove your manual line or page break.

Measure stretch

Many problems can arise when trying to make music look nice. One of these problems could be that the music is too crunched on the page. Another could be that a single measure or two flow onto another page. Both of these can be solved by adjusting the **measure stretch**.

The measure stretch is how tightly compressed or spread out the notes in a measure are. The other measures in the score will then be adjusted or moved automatically to accommodate for this extra space. The following figure shows different amounts of measure stretch applied to the same measure:

To change the measure stretch for one or more measures, first we select them, similarly to how we selected measures when we were copying and pasting them. Then we go to the **Layout** menu and click on **Add More Stretch** or **Add Less Stretch**. It is also possible to do this via the keyboard shortcuts. If one or more measures are selected, { adds less stretch and } adds more.

Beaming

The proper beaming of notes is a key feature of quality engraved scores that often goes unappreciated. It is extremely easy to change the beaming patterns to enhance the readability of your score. There are several utilities in the palette that allow for this.

To start, go to the section of the palette labeled **Beam Properties**. Hovering over each icon will tell you what it does. These properties can be applied to different notes. The **Start beam** option is for notes in the middle of an existing beam. It breaks the existing beam at the specified note, and starts a new beam on that note. The **Middle of the beam** option will ensure that the selected note is beamed to the notes on both sides of it, and the **No beam** option will break any beams going to the selected note.

Let's learn how to use these with a simple use case scenario. Suppose you enter three eighth notes followed by an eighth rest. MuseScore will automatically choose the following beaming:

However, to a musician who is sight-reading, it may be easy to confuse this with a triplet. To correct this, simply drag the **No beam** icon on top of the third eighth note in the passage. The note should highlight red as you hover over it, before you drop it. Once you let go of the mouse button, MuseScore will automatically adjust the beam according to what you specified.

Similarly, choosing the beaming wisely can make difficult passages easier to read. Let's consider the case of two sixteenth notes followed by two eighth notes and two more sixteenth notes.

Especially with the sharps and flats in this example, it would not be easy to sight-read such a passage. However, dragging the **Start beam** option on top of the B♮ makes this passage much cleaner and easier to read.

To undo any of these changes, ensure that you are not in Note Entry mode, and click on the note that you have changed. Then, in the **Beam Properties** section of the palette, double-click the **A** icon to reset it back to default.

Though MuseScore uses standard conventions for whether to put the beam above or below the notes, if you would like to change this, simply ensure that you are not in Note Entry mode, click on the beam, and press the *X* key. The beam will flip to the other side of the staff.

Grouping instruments

One additional technique that well-prepared scores use to enhance readability is grouping related instruments together. Consider the following two examples:

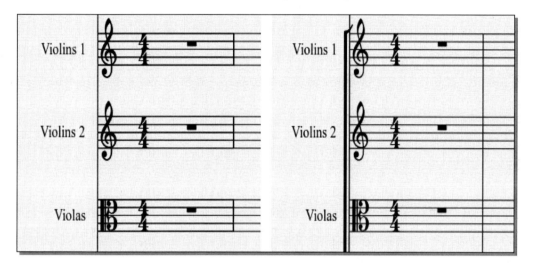

There are two differences between these two: the bracket on the left-hand side, and the extension of the barline throughout.

Extending the barline across multiple instruments is very simple. First, simply double-click on any barline of the first instrument in the group. A small blue box will appear at the bottom. Now just drag this blue box to the bottom of the last staff in the group. It should snap to the correct position. Now, clicking anywhere else in the score will finish editing the barline.

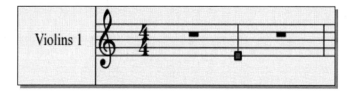

To create the bracket, locate the **Brackets** section of the palette. There should be two different bracket styles to choose from. Drag the square bracket onto the first staff in the group. It doesn't matter which measure you add it to in this staff, as MuseScore will know what to do.

Now, the bracket should be attached only to this instrument. This is not very useful, since brackets group multiple instruments, so let's double-click on the bracket. This will cause another blue box to appear, similar to when we were adjusting the barlines. Drag this down to the bottom of the last instrument in the group. It should snap to the correct place. Clicking anywhere else will finish editing the bracket. To delete the bracket later, just single click on it and press the *Delete* key.

Extracting parts

Now that we have finished working on our score, we need some way to give musicians their own copy of the music to perform. This is accomplished by extracting the parts. For practice, let's create a sample score with a clarinet, a cello, a piano, and a mezzo-soprano. Once you have done this, to extract the parts, go to the **File** menu and click on **Parts**. You should see the following screen:

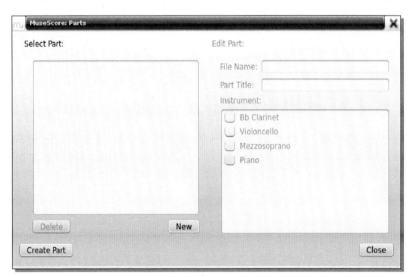

On the left, we have a list of the parts that are to be created. Right now, there are no parts yet. Let's create a part for the clarinet player by clicking on the **New** button, typing `clarinet_part` into the **File Name** field, and `Clarinet` in the **Part Title** field. The **File Name** is the default name that will be used when saving this part, and the **Part Title** is what it will show at the top of the page to denote this part. (For instance, if we were composing this for a clarinetist named Artie, we could write `Artie` as the part title instead.) Then, since we only want the clarinet staff to appear in this part, we check the **Bb Clarinet** box on the right-hand side. That's all there is to it!

Now, let's create another part for the cellist using the same method. Don't forget to check the **Violoncello** checkbox after filling in the title and file name! We should now have the following:

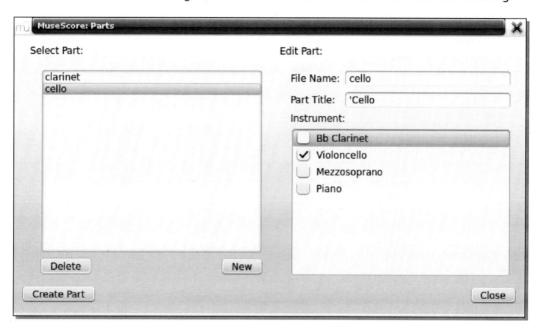

We can also create parts with multiple staves on them. For instance, it is usually nice to have a piano-vocal part instead of just a piano or vocal part. So, let's click on the **New** button again, and fill in `piano-vocal` for the file name and `Piano-Vocal` for the part name. Then, if we click on both the **Mezzosoprano** and the **Piano** checkboxes, the part will contain both!

When you have finished, click on each part in the new list you have created and press **Create Part**. As you do, each part should open in MuseScore as a new tab. You can click on each one individually, change the formatting if you would like, and print them by selecting **Print** from the **File** menu.

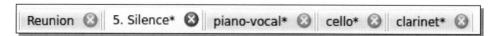

Note that there are asterisks on the tabs of all of the new parts. Each part must be formatted (if necessary) and saved individually. Just extracting the parts is not enough to save them. Notice that once you close the **Parts** dialog, the score will also have an asterisk. If you save the score, it will save your settings for extracting parts to make things easier in the future.

Congratulations, and welcome to the world of MuseScore! You now have the skills necessary to notate music using one of the leading pieces of music notation software in the world. The next section has some resources that may be helpful to you in going forward and taking the next steps.

People and places you should get to know

If you need help with MuseScore, here are some people and places that will prove invaluable.

Official sites

- **MuseScore.com** is a service that allows you to upload your scores to MuseScore Connect, interactively play back scores from your web browser, and discover new music from others. It is available at `http://musescore.com`.

- The **MuseScore Youtube How-to** page contains instructional video tutorials on both basic and advanced topics. It is available at `http://www.youtube.com/user/musescorehowto`.

- The **MuseScore Twitter** page will keep you updated on the latest news about MuseScore, and is available at `http://twitter.com/musescore`.

Articles and tutorials

- The **MuseScore Handbook** is a good first place to go if you have a question about something not in this book or you need clarification of a feature mentioned here. It is available at `http://musescore.org/en/handbook`.

- The **MuseScore How-to** page can be helpful if you need to know how to do less common notation tasks which are beyond the scope of this book and the MuseScore Handbook. It is available at `http://musescore.org/en/howto`.

- The **Development** page explains how to contribute to MuseScore as a translator, beta tester, writer, or programmer. It is avaliable at `http://musescore.org/en/development`.

Community and resources

- The **MuseScore Forums** are a helpful resource if you have any questions that are not answered by this book, the Handbook, or the How-to page. You can also suggest new features, get advice, and discuss MuseScore in general. It is available at `http://musescore.org/en/forum`.

- The **MuseScore Player for Android** allows you to play back MuseScore files on your smartphone, and access online scores. It is available at `https://play.google.com/store/apps/details?id=com.musescore.player`.

Thank you for buying

Instant MuseScore

About Packt Publishing

Packt, pronounced 'packed', published its first book *"Mastering phpMyAdmin for Effective MySQL Management"* in April 2004 and subsequently continued to specialize in publishing highly focused books on specific technologies and solutions.

Our books and publications share the experiences of your fellow IT professionals in adapting and customizing today's systems, applications, and frameworks. Our solution based books give you the knowledge and power to customize the software and technologies you're using to get the job done. Packt books are more specific and less general than the IT books you have seen in the past. Our unique business model allows us to bring you more focused information, giving you more of what you need to know, and less of what you don't.

Packt is a modern, yet unique publishing company, which focuses on producing quality, cutting-edge books for communities of developers, administrators, and newbies alike. For more information, please visit our website: www.packtpub.com.

Writing for Packt

We welcome all inquiries from people who are interested in authoring. Book proposals should be sent to author@packtpub.com. If your book idea is still at an early stage and you would like to discuss it first before writing a formal book proposal, contact us; one of our commissioning editors will get in touch with you.

We're not just looking for published authors; if you have strong technical skills but no writing experience, our experienced editors can help you develop a writing career, or simply get some additional reward for your expertise.

Getting started with Audacity 1.3

ISBN: 978-1-84719-764-1 Paperback: 220 pages

Create your own podcasts, edit music, and more with this open source audio editor

1. Teaches basic techniques for using Audacity to record and edit audio tracks - like podcasts and interviews

2. Combines learning to use software program with the simple theories behind digital audio and common audio terms

3. Provides advanced editing techniques and tips for using Audacity beyond a first project

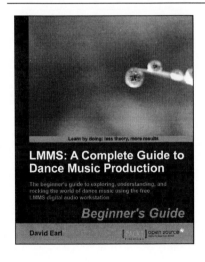

LMMS: A Complete Guide to Dance Music Production

ISBN: 978-1-84951-704-1 Paperback: 384 pages

The beginner's guide to exploring, understanding, and rocking the world of dance music using the free LMMS digital audio workstation

1. Create the dance music you wanted. An experienced guide shows you the ropes.

2. Learn from the best in dance music; its history, its people, and its genres.

3. Learn the art of making music: from the way you set up your equipment, to polishing up your final mix

Please check **www.PacktPub.com** for information on our titles

3D Game Development with Microsoft Silverlight 3: Beginner's Guide

ISBN: 978-1-84719-892-1   Paperback: 452 pages

A practical guide to creating real-time responsive online 3D games in Silverlight 3 using C#, X?BAP WPF, XAML, Balder, and Farseer Physics Engine

1. Develop online interactive 3D games and scenes in Microsoft Silverlight 3 and XBAP WPF

2. Integrate Balder 3D engine 1.0, Farseer Physics Engine 2.1, and advanced object-oriented techniques to simplify the game development process

3. Enhance development with animated 3D characters, sounds, music, physics, stages, gauges, and backgrounds

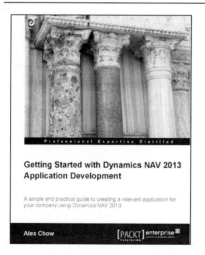

Getting Started with Dynamics NAV 2013 Application Development

ISBN: 9781-8-4968-948-9   Paperback: 230 pages

A simple and practical guide to creating a relevant application for your company using Dynamics NAV 2013

1. Understanding user requirements and drawing inspiration from existing functions

2. Creating the application and integrating it into standard Dynamics NAV

3. Presented in a simple tutorial style, with a resource to get a free trial full version to help you get started

Please check **www.PacktPub.com** for information on our titles